Crossing

Crossing

POEMS

Dean Olson

2012 · Fithian Press, McKinleyville, California

Printed in the United States of America

"The Spoon" was first published in *Prairie Schooner,* 2011.
"Quinault Rain Forest" was first published in *Atlanta Review*, 2012.
"Coming and Going" and "Filling the Stillness" were first published in *Innisfree Poetry Journal*, 2011.
"Wonder Woman" and "Window Shopping" were first published in *vox poetica* and *unbound CONTENT*, 2011.

Published by Fithian Press
A division of Daniel and Daniel, Publishers, Inc.
Post Office Box 2790
McKinleyville, CA 95519
www.danielpublishing.com

Distributed by SCB Distributors (800) 729-6423

LIBRARY OF CONGRESS CATALOGING-IN-PUBLICATION DATA
Olson, Dean Francis.
Crossing : poems / by Dean Olson.
p. cm.
ISBN 978-1-56474-535-4 (pbk. : alk. paper)
I. Title.
PS3615.L7337C76 2012
811'.6--dc23
2012014702

to Dena and Toska

Contents

Crossing

A Virtuous Peace

Years, and the time has finally come,
the state of calm for which he waited.

It feels as if his children are in bed asleep,
everything is in place and he can slip away.

His life becomes a flowing sheet,
much as the hospital curtain drawn around him
brings a sense of occasion, a singularity,
a silent extravagance.

Thoughts fill in as he remembers
the Pacific mist wetting his face,
the muffled sweep of aged dune grass,
the whispering surf,

glimpses granted at the edge of life
like graveyard stone rubbed to faintness
stakes its claim anew in damp air.

Unfinished Future

for Layne and Sulli

How satisfying
to imagine the range,
the full reach of unfinished future
ringing in the sound of my grandchildren
as they race through the house,
simply being.

How fulfilling
to imagine the promise of their season,
the welcome sound of their coming
like a flock of young geese settling in the field,
flyways subtly charted
in the yoke of their memory,

yet quick to shift and alter,
kite and veer, brake or go
if faced with uncertainty,
all the while leaving
scent of my passage.

The stroke of a brush,
a line of verse,
an existential note,
will be quite enough,
and though my palm is full of dirt
I will get up,
the whole of me alive again.

Red Plaid Pendleton

Brushing past it in the closet
brought me closer than I liked
so it hung in an unlit corner.

I wondered why I kept it,
why we didn't donate it to the church
with his other clothes
and how it came to be in my closet.

A weak moment paid for
with the smell of stale smoke,
the memory of him
leaving with Mom to Grange dances,
a stiff nip of bourbon loosening
the leased-out knot of muscled tension,
another shot easing the sinew of worry
before he pushed his thick arms in,
shouldered his way in,
put his arm around her waist.

In twenty years the smell
slowly grew meager, then gone,
the fabric letting him go.
Now I wear his Pendleton.

After a glass or two of wine
I feel a like a resurfaced road
with an old layer of rock beneath,
a deeper down place
where there is no slack, no give.
A place of work and worry
hidden on Saturday nights
by the warm glow of red plaid.

Permission

It is one thing to welcome
the ratcheting sound
of the anchor's windlass

absorbed in the promise
of each day
like greeting a new friend,

firmly grounded in knowing
who and where you are,
with plenty of line left in you.

It is another to fear the shift
of known ground beneath you

having lost the verve
and wit of youthful awareness,

for that matter,
having lost yesterday.

All the more reason to hoist
and go farther
than you ever expected possible,

light-headed and thin-boned
yet amazed by your boldness.

Awake, nimble in mind, free

as the heartbeat of a bird.

Gift of Life

Sounds like calf-suckling
each time he lifts a boot
leaving pools that blossom
muddy brown flowers.

Stride half his I hurry to keep up
facing into the mud, the bouquets,
away from hills barely visible
through blow and rain,
the river flooding low pasture.

Mud-flowers hurry to edges
raised by his boots as if rushing
to reefs of storm-lashed lagoons

Look up, he said, *we need to find her,*
she's down with calving,
likely drowning with the trying.

Exhausted from the work of it
she lies at the edge of a ditch.

We finish what she couldn't,
pull the dead calf from her,
get her up to stagger
at the end of a loose halter.

The river fills in behind us,
the work of our pulling
clings to the red mud,
whispers lap the shore.

Tasting at the Farmer's Market

She circles berries arrayed in little baskets.
It is late in the season, she needs to be careful.
It has happened before—mold could lie beneath
the topmost layer. She has learned
to take a second and third look,
taste deeper layers before committing.

A tall thin man pauses
to sample sliced apple at the next stall.
Afternoon sun highlights the color and clarity of his cheeks.
She looks for subtle gradations
that might hint maturity and character,
gains a rough measure of leg
from his tendency to cling to the sides of apple bins.

She passes close, subtly noses him
with little expectation of scented flowers, fruit or herbs,
simply to guard against the disappointing odor
of musty basement or wet wardrobe.
She knows a complete tasting requires her tongue,
that eventually a bold chewing would be needed
to assess body, fullness and depth.

Part of the pleasure lies in the possibility
she will find surprising complexity
and firm texture beneath the topmost layer;
that she might one day discover lingering finish and length.

But it is late in the season,
well past the springtime of exploration,
the time for taking chances.
She moves on to sample fall plums.

Elk

I go soft-eyed
seeing settled layers
of morning dew.
Never fail to feel young,
grow evermore expectant,
waiting
the opening curtain.

It would be too much
at my age
to say I am exuberant,
but nearly so,
nearly so.

As once at a friend's farm
I rose jubilant
seeing layers of mist
raise elk

from a field of white limbo.

They came and went,
given then retaken by the mist
like substance split,

at first undecided,
then erupting,
to reveal all that had been
in shafts of sun,

the abandoned spaces

emptying into me to keep.

Morning Cove

First-light makes morning
as I settle into the unfinished work
of dreaming a lifetime away.

Cockpit scuppers drip a chorus of leaky kitchen plumbing.
Morning breeze starts ripples on the hull
like cat tongues lapping milk
and the anchor chain snorts against the hawse
like a hungry pig.

A sail flaps like a chicken-house door,
and the rig sings like a robin.
Coiled line scrapes the mast like a dog at the door
while the bilge pump empties
as if a cow's bladder, and the dinghy drags
the bulwarks crowing like a rooster.

It seems the entire world ekes and crows
and I am lying in on my attic cot
waiting rustlings in the kitchen,
the low voice of our cow in the barn,
the decided slap of Dad's suspenders
on his thick shoulders.

Attic

My brothers and I lived
in steep-roofed, close-peaked attics
where the rarely used, the excess,
the in-the-way if left downstairs things
were given the gray dust
and musty smell of waiting.

It was a place where summer sweat
transformed comic book heroes
into wrinkled prunes
and winter breath fell to the floor.

But the sun greeted us before anyone else,
we could see across hay fields
and the rain and wind were roommates
inches above our heads.

Low, closed in, always looking down
as if hidden in the crotch of a cherry tree,
on lookout, unseen and seeing.
Bird-like, barn-loft high and dry,
above ground mist,
clear-headed and self-possessed,
identifying visitors before doors opened
and voices were heard.

First Up

Oh to be first up again.

First to follow pheasants
onto untouched dew,

to be the still center
of pasture waste lost in mist

silence holding back dawn
aching to bare its neck

my in-placeness caught
in a freak of sunshine
on whitewashed stem and stalk

as extravagant light enters
known and sure.

Stranded

From a distance she looked
like a beached log of perfect proportion,
a native symmetry traced
smooth and equal-sided,
belonging, yet out of place.

The wind lifted a hand
smelling of life at sea

but there was no flow or go,
a stiffening body
the surf would raise and roll,
the ebb would dress in ashen silt.

Unspoiled and round as new
she became the stuff of public muse,
dog-sniffs and kid-pokes, skirl of gull,
her life-taker a mystery to mull,
a phantom housed in the offing,
clothed in white stirred-up sea.

She came and went with the tide.
We watched her body alter
as if attending a wake
until we could bear watching no longer
and the undertaker took her aside.

Blue Mornings

In November, the blue predawn lasts for hours.
The moon's old face, the little of it she shows,
is washed-out weary gray. She keeps it hidden
behind clouds as if her work is already finished.
The decay of autumn waits in slimy layers
of molded yellow and red to be scrubbed
colorless as gray shirts beaten on stone.
Deer wait quiet and patient as ghosts
under orchard trees for shrunken apples.
A shoulder-high vapor clings to the wet ground
swallows the deer in suspended murk.

The bone-deep chilled language of Northwest rain
pounding my kitchen's single-pane windows
will slowly fill the crawlspace a foot
beneath me, raise inexorably to flood the drain field,
soak pasture until it becomes impassable bog.

This is only the beginning of winter's blue mornings
and I am accustomed to how they enclose me,
how they raise the well of melancholy.
So I take myself elsewhere writing this poem,
hold it in my warm hands to keep my spirits
above ground-water, put something fresh in the air,
like spring.

Rabbit

At twelve I enrolled in a program
teaching rural kids healthy living.
I fed and watered rabbits,
learned to pull their soft fur down
releasing a sweet-scented warmth,
the last of life rising in cold air.

In a few weeks the ghosts of
cooked rabbit overwhelmed our house,
slathered wallpaper with a saccharine
perfume, a thin-layered heftiness
as enduring as clabbered buttermilk
on a milk house floor.
We came to hate everything rabbit.

We were eaters of free range venison
sliced into steaks, ground, cut into roasts,
cooked in gravy and canned in mason jars.
Cellar shelves lined with canned venison
lifted our spirits, assured us we would winter fine.
"We're sitting pretty," Dad would say
as he closed the cellar door, our world
in proper balance.

At seventy-three I live in town, can't bring myself
to buy the tough gamy venison served
in tony restaurants. Deer living in ravines
and brushy slopes trace nightly circuits though
my neighborhood. They are used to me.
We're on good terms.

Labor Intensive

for Jill

Some work needs more labor than tools
and moves around to find the right mix.
This is why some work locates
where labor is plentiful while others
stay put, bound as they are to place
or market. Farmers are tied to pasture
and garden, fishers to particular grounds
and though their work costs more
it is trendy to favor neighbor over stranger.
I am in agreement, always patronize locals
sometimes sacrificing my yearning for grapes.
Just yesterday I shared my elevator
with a young woman caught in the rain.
She dripped like a raspberry waiting to be picked,
her sleeveless blouse clinging to uninhibited breasts,
pert nipples aroused by the rain's touch.
We laughed at the serendipity of local weather
and I caught myself leaning into the sheer
circumstance of place, drawn by the image
of a couple riding the plains. Caught in a storm
they dry themselves in a deserted line cabin
beneath a single blanket while their clothes
dry by the fire, the ultimate in neighborly sacrifice.

Reclamation

Skokomish Valley

I grew up in this valley, the one
I drive through when I've nothing
better to do. Once home to cows,
fields of timothy and broom
are overrun with sedge and thistle,
burly clumps of untamed orchard grass.
The apple orchard, barn and cellar,
the worn path to the creek,
the house my brothers and I lived
our way into consciousness are gone.
The tired two-room school building
lingers as grange hall and flea market.
The narrow blacktop sags into saturated soil
and the roadside store where I leaned across
the counter to touch a neighbor girl's tongue
is stubby willow.

Something massive, irrational and powerful
is happening. The river running through it
is taking the valley back in half my lifetime.
Everywhere I look life is temporary, obedient,
circumspect, cupped in suspense. People invest little
in the rich bottom land. Folks here travel light,
enter the valley only to feed
looking over their shoulder like migrant farmers
as the mountains watch in silence,
sentinels intent on having the last word.

Walking Upright

A friend asks why I walk bent over,
am I worried about a hard winter,
sickness in the family,
or simply studying
the uneven sidewalk as it rises
to tree roots like water to shore?
He argues it is summer,
men should walk upright in the sun,
my family is healthy
and the sidewalk is smooth.
I tell my friend it is as if I stand
in a small boat and must lean forward
to preserve stability in rough water,
that the wind may pick anytime
to rupture the thin membrane of calm.
Even now my pension is near capsize,
my home is underwater
and the tide that lifts all boats
is moored in banks
whose turnstiles I lean against
hoping to slip inside.
I tell my friend I lean forward
to brush warm moments of memory
like pieces of bread,
searching for something
that has disappeared,
a ship that is leaving without me.

Indulgences

> *like one returning who has swum below*
> *to free the anchor that has caught its hooks*
> *on a reef or something else the sea conceals*
> *spreading out his arms, and doubling up his legs*
> —*Dante,* Inferno, *Canto XVI, lines 133–136*

When I get depressed by endless rain
the moon cannot silence at night,
nor the sun dry by day, it seems
as if I am anchored prune-skinned
at the edge of an unchanging sea.
It must have been on such a day
half a millennia ago Luther posted his scribbles
proclaiming the door to heaven open to faith
and no one need pay with coin.
Imagine the flood of relief learning
one could actually pray into paradise
and do it without a paid guide.
So would it trouble him
to hear the faithful murmur
in chambered confessionals,
pour coin over the lip of coffers
to insure the turnstile opens,
as score keepers with open palms
leaven heavenly light from heights
exalted, rarified and heady?
And seeing how it is soil-turners, fishers
and chore women are let in now and then
to ratify an off-the-shelf hereafter,
a moment in the front row, a crust of bread,
a sip of wine in noble company,
wouldn't he fit in?
He could shrug his ample shoulders
into a new purple stole, tie the sainted
cord round his laced alb of linen
and be right back in business, tax free.

Love

No line
could sound the bottom,
plumb the fathoms of its depth.

No soap or warm water
could loosen
the ring forever bedded,
dampen candled memory.

And even now,

as confusion
coarsens his mood
and he turns from her,

she holds his worn hand,
remembers how the lamp glowed
when unfenced love spread
flush in spring.

Private Time

It was my favorite hidden place,
a grainy green-leafed unroofed tower.

Under me on one side
the steep roof of my attic bedroom,
our white house and worn porch.
On the other, the wood shed,
concrete-sided milk room and barn.

High in the cherry tree, above life itself,
fenced glebe and river gleam.

If a car turned into our driveway,
seclusion granted seniority of first sight
and I assumed the out-of-reach sideways glance
of the lofty, listening to every word,

as when in visitation my teacher graded
me a dreamer and window gazer
indifferent to text or paddle
and mother tilted a secret smile skyward.

On Being Elder

> *At last we touched upon the lonely shore*
> *that never yet has seen its waters sailed*
> *by one who then returned to tell the tale*
> *—Dante,* Purgatory, *Canto I, lines 130–132*

I left any sense of creeping privilege at work
when I retired, or lost it elsewhere.
I longed for a community where elders
were sought out, made the center of things,
listened to. I envisioned telling stories to children
gathered at my feet. Tapping the reservoir of wisdom
ambassadors from the past are thought to possess,
I would draw lessons from folktales to mark
important life passages, carve moral boundaries.
But everywhere I looked the young
were like surfers mounting the crest of each moment,
riding the rush and lift of satellite and network.
Few had time to feel the slow steady pull of life,
enjoy the ordinariness of it, the pleasing work in it.
I came to see eldership as a no where,
an island no one willfully puts in, a strand
above high water where elders lie beached.
As I drew closer, I felt the sun's warmth,
noticed how it is elders glow as with the all-over
tan of the unclad, lament nothing,
lay aside the burden of emotional weight
to tend one another with a caring that asks
nothing in return, needing nothing more.

A Dread Unnamed

A few years before he died
dad said "we were poor" as if
the thought was new, a realization
he had come to for the first time.
This seemed odd to me.

We had always been poor,
never wholly at ease.
We lived a quiet caution that held us still
as if an unnamed dread had hold of us,
could reach into the house
and take what we had.
There was no place to run,
no place to hide,
no alternative to how it was for us.

I came to understand
this is what country poor feel.
It isn't paraded around city streets.
It is a quiet thing one grows so used to,
it seems ordinary.

At Water's Edge

for Azriel James Carver, age 8
lost at sea 2010, Olympia, Washington

His mother drove
the rutted curve into the bay,
confused or sacrificial,
taking Azriel to a faraway place
beyond puzzled love.

I pull the kenneled boy
from his cold water-grave
as the car fills
and his chill-whitened hands tremble
beneath the sweeping flood,
slowly close in dreamlike disbelief.

And as he glimmers away
exiled to that elsewhere
cargo children are taken,
a place of vigils, solitudes and tears
where the lantern's wick dies,

I pilot my wherry to his side,
a celestial linkman a-coming
to ferry his weightless frame
to the warm forever of small mudlarks
where soft voices whisper.

Blowing Stumps

Hearing thunder I become expectant,
feel my body tense

and I am thirteen waiting
for the shattering sound of torn wood,
remembering how my brothers and I
leaned into gnarled stubbornness
prying between roots with steel points,
lying flat for the last of it.

We stood by as Dad taped dynamite
into a bundle, pressed the bronze cap
and primer cord into the center stick.
He tamped the hole, lit the cord
then waited, seeing it take
before running.

The earth jumped unexpected,
the sky filled with splinters and smoldering bits
smelling of ancient musk and scorch,
then everything lapsed ordinary.
We pressed in, picking roots
wisping smell of powder,
scraped everything clean,
breaking ground for cows.

Third Hand

No one talks much
in the food bank line.
Faces tend from one another,
garrisoned inside weathered collars.

I want each of them to trust
the tether of their indigence,
see in it a hand-hold for troubles
outside their making, a quiet lying-in
waiting the storm to settle.

As offshore when the sea sweeps
stem to stern and sailors are held
by the third hand,
a strong tether made fast
to lines binding least to most,
showing the way to keep going,
the whole being worth it.

A Sense of Occasion

A sense of occasion
came over us
when the deep-bellied beam
touched the pier

and firmly made,
our faces flushed with sun and wind
we went below out of it.

The sea playing its tape,
I leaned against the galley
like a bar at the pub.

You sidled up
changing the entire course of the day
as evening,
gaining its first hold,
came upon us fully fledged.

Harold and Isaac

Fishing Weaver Creek
summer mornings when night
fades into day,
sitting on a low bridge

pleased to be first out of the attic,
first to try trout living under logs
dangling moss thin as lace,

I coax crawlers under shaded logs
hoping rainbow with names
will think worms fall from moss

as a doomed muskrat comes to sniff
apple slices on a stick
placed there by my brother
who wants a Plymouth coupe.

A stone-faced heron watches the muskrat
with one plumed eye,
the other tilted at me
until awkwardly, improbably, she lifts,
twists, turns, climbs, croaking a racket,

as the muskrat reaches for a slice
and the sun makes my shadow,
keeping Harold and Isaac under lace.

I stay on,
fulfilled by what might have been,
repelled by what was.

A Keeper Only

after Walden, *Henry David Thoreau*

As a young man
the smell of fall drew me
and I thought myself a hunter,
now find I am not.

Years later I thought myself
a fisher and longed for the pull
of the taut line, but each year
I am less a fisherman.

Now, feeling you all-round,
I know I am not center
but mere subscript, visitor,
a keeper only.

after Love's Ripening, *Rumi*

I don't see myself
as living in submission.
I feel my soul fully fledged,
the eggshell of my body broken.

It is as if I have wandered a desert
sailing my boat on dry land
and now an old man,

the sky is a garden of roses,
thistles are flowers, rocks are gems
and sunrise is a ripe orange.

In Springtime

I knew you in the springtime
of days given to fantasy and firmness
when in a single breath we came unhinged
inspired by the song and touch
of nakedness in darkened gardens.

Now I am a ripened grape
the furnace of my belly filled
with toast and wine, my opened shirt
a drying tombal of setting sun
falling out of love with love.

I don't lament how waves of desire
once wet the sand of distant beaches,
what could be or might have been.
Memory is warmed by your touch
and in my heart you dwell.

The Work

after A. Pushkin, The Work,
V. Nabokov, Verses and Versions, *139*

My long work done, I stand
as a day laborer might stand
wages in hand vacantly staring
into tomorrow's uncertain light
waiting with silent companions
long evening and hollow night.

I meditate the unbroken hours
until thoughts are written down,
then go about oddly stimulated,
as if convinced some secret things
have overnight been settled.

Taking Time

One must press close to the ground
to hear the small voice of a vole,
feel the weighted shudder of distant hoofs,
smell the incomprehensible freedom of decay.

And you need to sit quietly
to sense the air thickening with night,
gather about you the compelling silence of stars.

Take the measuring pace in passing, notice
how the promise of rain-tongues raises children's faces,
falling snow dampens the sound of browsing deer,
how a chorus of tree frogs pauses.

Take these senses into yourself
traveling beyond the sheltering touch of skin.
Lean into the thigh-deep evening mist,
swallow handfuls, begin the heart-work
of weathered seasons, seedbed of dreams.

Taking Air

Taking air on deck I see the moon
high and preposterous.
Old work whore,
lozenge of love trapped in the sky,
your hard white face peers through hoards of clouds
as mine stares back from the black sea.

I know you as the giver of tide and time,
the seaway lumina I steer at night,
the candela of current.

Elsewhere you are the love medallion
churning young hearts
beneath your color of fermented buttermilk,
whose restless glands you lift
warm and flushed,
spread-out and unbuttoned.

To each of us you are the giver of right-of-way
lighting the path of depth and go,
your breasts an open-work we sense through our skin,
a shared calling of blood;
the swollen youth taking their pleasure in tall grass,
me plumbing your wide stare.

Sleepers

We lie in on a brisk spring morning
inhaling heaven gathered like a thing
in sheets smelling of outdoors.

Like slivers of dreaming sun
the girls join us, entangling
swung-open legs in our warmth.

We listen to their measured breathing,
how it is as with gull stalled in a breeze,
the sea below wild in foam and froth,
they use the minimum

as if someone deep inside has told them
to conserve and build for the hour
when honed and made ready
they leave to weigh the day.

We feel how it is they are still in wrapping paper,
thin-limbed doves rising in our hearts,
tender spring buds first-leafing in morning sun,

a man's world waiting outside our door.

Confession

Do I write
for the praise of visitors
or for those around whose kitchen table
I will be remembered?

Who can lay claim to the telling face
and would want from me more than they could keep
in the refining glimpse
of a faded album?

Among strangers I am veiled in mist.
My poems lack the clarifying sound of seabirds,
the lush sensuality of rain-sweetened cedar,
the form-rendering lick and touch of familiarity.

So I write for those I have loved,
a little spent with each poem,
sometimes seeing the end then moving on,
returning as if summoned

to that place where homespun voices
dress praise in bright ribbons
and I allow myself the thick ordinariness
of speaking in my own tongue.

It is here and only here I intersect,
deep-seated coordinates drawing me in without effort.
It is here no tariff is weighed,
the door is simply left open and I enter.

Counselor

for Layne

I imagine my father the one sitting
across this table,

my leaving-home suitcase packed
as yours is now,
oozing impatience;

his yellowed work-thickened fingers
knotted stiff
as he studied putting words together

then looking straight into me
making the point,
his tanned forehead rutted in the doing,

me hearing little
but this
above the nervous clamber to go;

"remember the sound and smell of this place,
everything about it
and you will keep away the unwanted things...

you will keep your head,
your feet touching the ground...

and what you do,
you will do on your own,
doing your own work,
no one else's...."

Album

I enjoyed your latest book of poems
one said, *they seemed to flow together*
as one linked to another, said the other,
you have found your voice, said a third.

And I rush to lift the pen,
leaning into the late night,
rising in morning when the deer bed,

writing for the ones
who have known me all along,
who will comfort me with warm hands
when the time comes.

I reach in, gather more,
feeling around in the thin cupboard of our kitchen,
the wood-heated living room,
the sloped-roof attic bedroom.

And out of thick-layered stuff
taken for granted and forgotten,
I glean the left-out, the left-over,
take them in and let them go

putting everything down in clean sheets,
the sound they make being everything.

Trolling

She strolled by as if let out.
The cobbled path flashed like river bottom
in the filtered shadow of overhead leaves.
I turned to her,

though it was time to leave,
intrigued by the intimate note she sang,
the witchery of trailing brightness,
the tight silver-veined wag. I stayed on

watching her appear and disappear,
glimpsed imagination playing itself out
then fleeing recklessly, as if helpless,
afraid, needy. I went to her,

the air roiled when we touched.
Loose-footed and free as never before
I found myself neither here nor there,
my heart caught off guard, opened.

Pressed Flowers

...my seeing became too large for speech
which fails at a sight beyond all boundaries
...although my vision is almost entirely faded,
droplets of its sweetness come...

—Dante, Paradiso, *Canto XXXIII, lines 52–66,*
trans. by Robert Pinsky

She picked poppies, columbine,
Monkshood and lily, violets and lupine,
Seeding hillside and field

In folded pages of old dictionaries, newspapers
Clamped under wood, Voltaire and Virgil
Pressed thin by washed brick

To return odorless and brittle, taking hostage
As they emerged from the dry undergrowth
Of duff-edged pages settled-on and fading.

And what was deep comes churning up,
Mute petals wing-open in airy currents
As if fresh-brushed by her finger tips

And seeing *becomes* too large for speech
As life impressed long ago spreads her spirit
Like melting frost glistens in morning sun.

Redeemed

In a dream-wish you came to me
seasoned and bendy,

to play with, lie about with.

And you said

you may do whatever you like
as long as you want. I have nothing
to hide and will teach you.

I glimpsed your jeweled gift,
haven in the flickering light,

a hand reaching from the jetty as I drifted,
my feet above the bottom,
fasted and shy in the mirror of nakedness.

You taught love without shame
in the glow of sunrise,
by candle light,
beneath moon glitter and in warm spring rain.

You took me by the hand,
showed how you were made,
how love could please,
how the feast rises to bursting
as ripe fruit plucked and eaten fresh from the tree.

Heated we lay back, redeemed,
wet and raised.

Writer's Block

At times verb and vowel
flow free as alder catkin
on the windy slope of spring.

Other times, it's like grafting
limb-upon-limb, coaxing,
teasing vowels from exile,

while verbs languish
like spent husks of autumn
slumber in winter's bin.

Go to the place river meets sea.
Loft dried twigs and kept dreams
into the eye of a peaked tepee.

Coddle a whispering flame
as if it is yeast in the kitchen
of your mother's cupped hands.

Let this memory warm you.
Vowel and verb will quicken,
and reborn will flow

from the estuary of your tongue
into the rippled sea,
write your name on the water.

Quinault Rain Forest

My steps spring from ruminant ground,
mold-thickened place-holder,
endless embalmer of time
moistened by twelve feet of rain each year.

I smell earth's pantry,
the nesting ground of vole,
sump of deer and rodent bone,
pollen-bin of moss and bracken.

My boots leave small pools of innocence
in the insatiable ground,
the broken thatch heals itself full-bedded

even before my sound fades
cabined beneath the confining canopy,
muffled in the lush wet of full-breasted rain.

Someday I will lie right here on the fingering ground,
composing my windfall song to the reclaimer,

an asylum seeker among the bracken and moss,
a whisper
in the thickening.

Cathedral

Step past roadside scotch broom,
sweep through hip-deep Oregon grape,
skirt patches of blazing fireweed,
straddle rotting windfalls,

enter the cathedral of shadow
where sound is filtered by ancient fires
recorded and reared in thick canopied pads,
where light fractures
in the stained-glass window of falling mist,

and in a short while, no time at all,
you are ready to travel anywhere
frail thought takes you

as you close your eyes,
inhale the ancient vapor,
open the wardrobe of centuries
and step inside.

Crawlspace

Named for the hand-and-knee ceiling
one found peering through the narrow opening,
the crawlspace brimmed
with the flow and perk of winter rain.

As a kid I would lift the hatch,
throw my arms across the gap,
hang suspended like a bridge
balancing the things that raise
with the things that let down,
my pale face hovering above the black,
spit rippling in dark circles.

I watched as spring formed
rivulets in the puddled muck,
the gradual coagulation and firming
turned earth into a kind of fermented buttermilk
that hardened and settled
into smooth gray clay.

Sunlight slowly swept our house
free of mold, telling us
we no longer stood inches above
the still pool of winter
which had finished us vulnerable
and strangely belittled.

Hosanna

A nevertheless sun
still south of east touches us
with a chilled glimmer.

Overnight sea-weight
has pressed the sand clay-smooth
leaving trench like spectral filled mounds.
Blanched roofs of clams
and disentangled crabs
mark endings,
trace the sea's comings and goings.

Clear running rivulets
flow to the sea in capillaries
we dip to wash the fretful parts of sleep
as if preparing ourselves

when out of the blue

we remember life without worry
and on the sea's fresh placement
imagine ourselves
new upon the scene
steady and fit as we are
for whatever comes.

Straightening

I want to witness the sea coming ashore
the whole of my life,
breathe her fresh whipped fragrance
lush with possibility.

I want to stand motionless before her,
walk slowly along the curve of her body,
bathe in the rainbow-hued mist,
listen to the compelling rhythm of her voice

as she rinses me of masquerade,
removes my masks of pretence,
straightens in me what the world has bent.

Scaling

The sea, athletic and moon-lit,
comes to forage.
Phosphorescence dances like a seductress
on carapace freckled sand.

A daughter stands in the circle of light
before knowing the names,
her mind sea-dipped in moon glitter.

Kelp pulls at her ankles,
the easy yielding puddle-places of her feet
urge furtherance, invite deepening.

An anchoring hand,
willful and unhindered, age harrowed and firm
reaches for her,
steadies her beyond the sea's hold
as she scales this place.

The Laboring Oar

I had no idea
the weight
of the laboring oar
she shouldered

until she laid it down,
left me alone,
out of my element
feeling the heft of it

pull against the thole
as the loom fell,
the blade found
its task,

and facing
into the work of it
my back to the wind,
I understood.

Crossing

As one by one the leaves fall off in autumn
Until at last the branch is bare and sees
All that was looted from it on the ground.
—Dante, Inferno, *Canto III, lines 112–4*

I would see my neighbor leave for work,
scissored hair and pressed slacks
filling the air with crisp urgency.
There was a steady straight aheadness about him,
a high velocity man brimming.

He retired last year, takes the dog
to a free-range park around noon
or wanders neighborhood streets.
His long hair and beard drip rain
in the letting-go leash-free life.

He gazes into the late winter gloom
certain he is missed as he slowly descends
the ladder leaning against his world.
The weight lifted, he is unburdened,
light-headed, dismayed, grounded.

Cellar Errand

If you ask have I felt the quick pounding of a heart,
the rising firmness of a fear-swollen tongue,
I remember the root cellar where mother stored summer.
The faded shake roof peered from orchard grass
like the gray wings of a giant bird.
Narrow stone steps led down to a heavy cedar-planked door
fastened to buried log walls by crude hammer-tormented hinges.
A feeble knob-and-tube web-screened light
spread thick capes of darkness over burlap bags
of unwashed potatoes smelling like freshly dug graves.
Apples wrapped in blood purple tissue loomed
like swollen bruises, jars of skinned red tomatoes
sported yellow-veined flesh, peach halves
with gaping red sockets like those under fresh-pulled teeth,
and browned venison cooked in a cauldron
of flour-thickened gravy lined dusty shelves
that disappeared into the dark cellar.
The ancient rough-cut shelves were set-away from the walls.
Air moved slowly from the earthen floor to a small roof hole
capped by a slow turning finned hat that groaned
like rusted chain and sent flickering slices of light
into the dark. I felt the cellar's still cool dryness
as I stood in the half-light of earth listening
to murmurs and rustlings beneath the lowest, darkest shelves
trying to remember what I was there to fetch.

Small Harbor

She came in riding
the setting sun,
pushing a dark shadow
that filled the harbor.

She came in just as evening
brought trees down to play
in the water,

just as other boats finished shortening
anchor lines to swing clear,
just as lamps were being lit.

Everyone hoped she would find
no room and turn away, or, failing that,
would anchor near someone else.

But she dropped heavy tackle
and chain in the center
of the small harbor.

Like players rearranging
chess pieces after the Queen moves,
everyone settled in once again.

No light or sound came from her
as night wrapped the harbor around us.

It was as though a whale slept
in our middle-space.

We came to accept her as one of us,
grew strangely comforted
by her quiet being there,

with us, in the dark.

Innocence

It was the place of first touching.
Girls in crisp dresses huddled
in small groups across the wooden
floor, glancing quickly now and then
at the boys leaning with calculated
informality against the wall, hands finding
something to do in their pockets.

Parents stood aside, older farmers
and ample women sat on the few benches
left out. The saxophone was held up
with calving, but the fiddle, guitar, bass
and drums got things going with slow
waltzes, and a foxtrot now and then to set
a faster pace.

Mothers pressed gently on the backs
of sons and daughters, and gradually,
we touched hands, felt shoulders being clasped,
felt waists being held, sampled the scent
of one another as we slowly turned,
arms holding bodies far apart,
looking at our shoes.

Bartering

Marlene taught me bartering
on cold winter days
when school was closed for snow.
We sat on the floor behind the stove,
our legs stretched out,
backs leaning against the wall,
shoulders touching. I would bring
my stack of comic books, Marlene
would bring her bounty. We would
read for hours, grateful for the soft white
flakes gliding slowly past the windows.
When the spirit moved her,
Marlene would take my hand under her shirt
to the wonderful softness growing there.
She would kiss me on the cheek
while leaning over, my hand
cupped under her breast, her hand high
on my thigh, and take another comic book
for her take-home pile. I could never remember
which comic books she liked,
maybe it didn't matter that much.
After all, it was a snow day, I had found
a warm place behind the stove,
and Marlene was teaching.

Winter Spine

She thinks she feels the spine
of winter especially strong
this time. Then she remembers
many winters that startled
her in this way.

But just now it is as if
the spine is a needle
stitching her to the chair,
holding her there, keeping her
from winter walks.

She sees herself through
the window as
yellow verbena and yarrow
become bent and colorless
from cold.

Tomorrow, a wedge of winter sun
will wrestle warmth
through that window
to feed her spirit,
mend her body.

She will hold tight this time,
this warmth,
and later
she will tell children
the stories only the very old remember.

Wake Violation

Safety Inspection

It happened in bright sun and light chop,
the kind of day gull, heron and scooter
bathe in warmth, content with being.

We stopped her for speeding, creating
wake in a quiet area, an ordinary
oversight on a day

when the sharp edge of thinking
softens as if delighted by wind
brushing bare skin.

Nothing was ordinary about her composure
as she drew close to our flashing blue lights.
I remember even now

how the plunge-front tankini strained to hold
bronzed breasts as she leaned into working
our beam-ends tightly together;

how she used flotation vest pull handles
to avoid premature discharge of the appliance
until she wanted full firmness and resilience;

how she would excite fire extinguisher compounds
by gently pounding the narrow red cylinder
against her low-rise bottom, and how
she held flares erect to erupt in the night.

Just as I turned to examine her flame arrester,
thinking to explain its value in maintaining
smooth deliberate power,

just as we began to explore how poetry
could release her body to the soul of the sea,
the crew reported we had drifted into the shallows.

Sand Bar

Sand and sea breeze bring them here,
a strange mix, like old sailors on bar stools
in every beach town from Port Townsend
to San Francisco.

This stretch of coast is no different. Beach
Morning Glory binds odd sorts together,
then parades around the bar
showing off pink and purple petals
as if to toot her funneled horns.

Fleshy Glasswort feels under appreciated
in this crowd, bides time until called
to lay her green asparagus body
next to red snapper or golden curried chicken
in a chic San Francisco restaurant.

She wants to get far away from crude
sedges boasting their sex like spiked
adolescent hair. She smells the sweet ambrosia
of long life offered by Silver Burweed,
as though anyone in this crowd thinks
further ahead than the next round.

and no one appreciates the work of stately Sea Watch,
ever alert, barring the door to evil spirits.
I enjoy this odd collection of ne'er-do-wells,
come often to learn of rumors running
up and down the beach. I seem to fit right in.

Fiddlehead

You are innocent, fresh and sweet,
tucked tightly together
as roe in salmon,
showing tops of tender curled heads,
the length of your bodies whorled
in well laid coils
one nested within another
just inside the door.
The damp nourishes stems
of promise
as you gather strength, look around,
at first tentative, then impatient
to burst out,
stretch your legs in the spring sun.
Is it perverse
to peer the way I do,
watch you grow each day
as you come into view
green and supple,
judge as I do each day,
the time to take you home,
warm you,
place your young bodies on my bed of rice,
savor the taste of spring you keep inside?
I will offer a prayer,
uttered softly over red wine.

Window Shopping

Some of us give the window
little more than a sideways glance
that lingers.
A hurried upward lift of the eyes
that hesitates
as if startled seeing bright colored birds.

Others stop. Stand for a while.
Look, try to sort it out,
our eyes turning down
as we walk away distracted,
prying open the musty cupboards of love.

Some of us are like deer caught in headlights.
Our eyes widening,
uncertain what we were thinking of,
where we were going,
what we should do now we have been seen
standing here in plain view,
looking.

We are the world's old men
who walk past the lingerie window
as we wander downtown
for morning coffee
or walk the mall before shops open.

It may be the fishnet lacy cheek panty
with minimal back coverage
that rouses us from simple black coffee
to the risky double pump mocha
with whipped cream.

And certainly, it is the waist cincher thong
stirring our memories
of back-seat entangling,
the joint effort to press flesh to flesh,
that makes us want the cheese Danish.

The Spoon

You are a nice man, do you work here?
she asks, taking the spoon into her mouth,
the large signs above the bed warning
coma patient, choking risk, deaf.
I raise the spoon again
filled with strained vegetables
the color of carrots, or squash.
She opens her mouth and I lift
the spoon into it as I did
nearly thirty years earlier.
Signs and pictures tell her
You are twenty-seven. You have
a mother and father, a sister, a husband and baby,
anything else we think will ease her back.

Sometimes I expect her to grip the spoon in her mouth
and hold it as she once did,
her eyes gleaming with the fun of it,
then letting go.
I would smile, lower the spoon
to scoop drippings from her chin,
filling it to be gummed and held again in our little game.

But now she takes the spoon each time I touch her lips,
releases it,
and I ignore drippings falling to her bib.
She turns, *You are a nice man, do you work here*?
I explain again that I teach,
filling the spoon, lifting it,
hoping to gain another bite
....my dad is a teacher she says excitedly
looking at the picture wall, at me.
I know, I answer, *I am your dad.*
Oh, she says, turning to the spoon.

Boston Harbor Marina

South Puget Sound, Olympia, Washington

I come to this place
of unhurried beauty

and if it is a day I am given
to noticing—

see how it is
of everyone something is asked
what each can do is fitted,
no one is left carelessly alone,
how a seal comes to be named
and lives content in coddled sea
smelling thick of salt as sea should

and if it is a day I am given
to dreaming—

feel the sea wash thoughts
tinted with worry and want,
hold close caring
untouched by city life
made in this place of unhurried beauty
where everyone has a name
and no one is left apart.

Wonder Woman

At bedtime we tell our girls
how she uses the Lasso of Truth
to make evil men honest and obedient,
vambraces forged from Zeus' shield
to protect the innocent.

She is a model of goodness,
we say, tucking them in tight.
Unlike simple straight-ahead steroid heroes,
she pursues love, peace and sexual equality.

We tell of her strength, wisdom and cunning,
yet she is soft and tender, often laments
fighting evil leaves little time to visit her island home.

Noticing the absence of boys on the island
the girls ask *Is Wonder Woman gay?*
We say it doesn't matter.
Loving preferences would not keep her from fighting evil.
We tell them how she could be and do anything,
even if gay, so long as she told no one about it.

Their eyes closed around this truth,
forever knowing,
there are times honesty and goodness hold hands,
times they do not.

Coffin Berths

Built chest-high above line stowage,
narrow pew-shaped aft cabin berths
cribbed in thick planked leeboards
higher than the eye on a flattened body,
rimmed in wood worn smooth by years
climbing in, climbing out,

line the unlit cabin smelling as if the ship
is a funeral barge filled with hemp
and the decay of brine-soaked sailors
whose lifeless bodies lie interned inside
the planked cribs, ears shuttered
like the dead.

The deck watch, still as ghosts,
dumb and bleary as sodden timbers,
listen dreamily under the dim anchor light;
the groan of chain in the hawse pipe,
the gentle wash of tide against the hull
calling their turn.

And when the time comes,
there is absolutely no reluctance, none,
to lie deep in the latent heat of the last body,
the shadow of leeboards shuttering the unwanted;
the lull and sway of coddling sea,
the benevolent embrace of the cribbed coffin
closing round.

First Time

Her first time, eyes widen
to the heel of the wetted hull
throwing spume
as if she straddles a furrow-crazed beast.

Before fear harnesses her,
dries her mouth, swells her tongue;
before her young life becomes a blur
blinding her
to the heavenly pleasure of plunge, of lift;

I place her hand on the pulsating rudder,
her fingers around the strumming, rooted line.
She feels the long-tailed pull of moist purpose.
Gradually,
fear washes from her, color returns to her lips,

shoulders straighten, as she comes to understand
she was born fit, can take the strain.
She mounts the beast,
sails it into the brisk pull of night.

Forgetting Mother

Our daughter worries she will forget
the shape of your face,
the sound of your voice.
How you smelled tucking her in,
the tinge of salt on your lips.

I tell her not to worry.

In the quiet of bedtime,
the chatter above the clatter of dishes
or hushed disclosures over coffee,
she will remember
how you sounded fresh or weary,
smelled of garden soil or morning freshness.

She will hear you in the voice of children,
see you in her mirror of thoughtfulness.
Smell the sweetness of your body
in her morning bedding,
feel your skin when she bathes,
taste the salt of your tears when she cries.

I tell her forgetting you

is to misplace herself, not see or feel her children.
It would be as if
she could renounce the gentleness of spirit
that washes through her
and somehow guides her
into each tomorrow.

Leaving

He leans against the top rail,
elbows lodged tight as tent poles,
hands pressed to his cheeks,
toe-down boots healed to the bottom bar,
shoulders cold-hunched,
back arched over the gate

waiting the first burst of spring,
that slender slice of morning magenta
slow-blending to thickened red and yellow,
molten, drawing the upper limb of promise
from beneath blue soil.

Behind him winter's long-nursed rage
whips field stalk and nude alder
with lingering savagery
as the sodden earth waits
to firm-up, settle-in and green.

He lingers hove-to
as a thin rooted plant leans from wind
dreaming young dreams
beyond paying out hand-over-hand,
season-after-season,

until he is old enough to see
how life could be otherwise,
strong enough to follow the pull
as spring lifts the latch.

Coming and Going

I pass the winter-going of bracken,
the outer layer browning
bedding themselves down for their own good
and the good of the living;
lapping as they wane
encircling time in the pooled rain of winter.
Not at odds with anything,
simply finished
but for the pillowed seeding lying in wait
among disembodying fronds.

Faith is placed in me like the bracken,
daisies in grazed fields,
asters in hoof-trampled puddles.
I mix my withering bouquet with carnal spit,
and in the name of seasoned roundness,
gift the coming spring,
granting myself the last word.

Filling the Stillness

If you are not here when I get home,
sometimes I sit at the kitchen table
listening to the stillness.

After a while I bring in some wood,
start a fire, the crack of kindling sounding
like the door latch;

open a bottle of wine, watch it breathe
until the porch light senses its time
to push winter into the yard.

I will sit like this a while longer, the fire
a wall flicker, the porch light
a steady floor patch

until you fill the stillness, turn on the lights
and I busy myself unloading groceries.

It's not something a man likes to talk about.

Fall Walk

A light September breeze carried
my father's sweat and wood pitch smell
from the doe carefully picking
her way through salal and red huckleberry

so close we could hear the brush as she passed through
looking-up from the shadows now and then
to chew and spoon sound into large ears.

These were the smells he brought home each night
to thicken like soup in the kitchen heat,
stirred now and then by the even hand of his voice.

The doe stood quietly trying to make
sense of things when the wind changed,
and one evening took him with her

to return in fall as I walk with the heavy musk
of maple leaves, the acrid bite of fir pitch,
listening to the passing-through sound of salal and huckleberry
as it moves slowly aside and swiftly back.

Appalachian Egg Basket

Built to carry labor fragile and scarce,
high-handled like a hooped wood bin,
sized small as a kettle,

round sides, ribbed curves
of split oak tight woven in hand-sewn
shock-absorbing weaves.

Close-knit to carry the gathered-up,
give if dropped on steep gravel paths
from hen house to kitchen.

Buttocks shaped with a deep undercut
tucked like the opulent narrow crease
between plump cheeks astraddle a fence

keep morning eggs apart until raised
together by sure hands over hot bacon grease,
thumbed open and gently lowered in.